Beyond The Greener Pastures

The enthralling stories of five Ghanaian old school friends in London

Inspired by true life stories

Nana Ama Adu-Kwapong

Kingdom Publishers

Copyright© Nana Ama Adu-Kwapong 2024

All rights reserved. No part of this book may be reproduced in any form by photocopying or any electronic or mechanical means, including information storage or retrieval systems, without permission in writing from both the copyright owner and the publisher of the book. The right of Nana Ama Adu-Kwapong to be identified as the author of this work has been asserted by her in accordance with the Copyright, Designs and Patents Act 1988 and any subsequent amendments thereto.

A catalogue record for this book is available from the British Library.

All scripture quotations have been taken from the New International version of the Bible.

ISBN: 978-1-916801-14-1

1st Edition 2024 by Kingdom Publishers,

London, UK.

You can purchase copies of this book from any leading bookstore or email **contact@kingdompublishers.co.uk**

I'm grateful to God for the opportunity to write and to my family, for their encouragement and support.

Contents

November 2008	9
Chapter 1	9
Chapter 2	15
Chapter 3	21
Chapter 4	27
Chapter 5	33
Chapter 6	39
Chapter 7	47
August 2023	53
Chapter 8	53
Chapter 9	61
Chapter 10	67
Author's Profile	75

November 2008

Chapter 1

It's a soggy Friday afternoon in November 2008 and I am sitting in a coffee shop near Waterloo station in London with four old school mates Akua, Susan, Abena and Sharon nursing a cup of hot chocolate since I have still not gotten used to drinking tea or coffee. It's been over twelve years since we all got together and the excitement is palpable in our voices as we talk and giggle about when we were in boarding school; St Philomena's Girls Secondary School (High School) in Accra, Ghana. In fact, for a moment, it was as if we were back in our student dormitories prattling about how we couldn't wait to graduate from secondary school; but the cool chill in the air and the pitter-pattering of the rain outside, which is by any standards not tropical, gave me a chilling reminder that I was no longer in Ghana, and jostled my mind back to the café.

"So, what have you all been up to since we last met?" I asked. A flippant question, thrown in without much thinking and everyone laughed heartily. Laughter that I later realized was hiding a lot of pain and regret for some and pride at great achievements for others.

My name is Afua. I am thirty-one years old and have been living in London for the last eight years. I would like to introduce you to Susan. She is also thirty-one and has been living in London for eight and a bit years. Susan left Ghana with great plans to further her education. She had received admission to study for a Master's degree in International Relations at a Russell Group University in the UK. She was ecstatic when she received her admission letter and after a grueling session at the British High Commission in Accra, she was given her student visa. The search for greener pastures, far beyond the borders of Africa motivated several people, both young and old to subject themselves to very intrusive visa application processes that often involved a questioning process worse than sitting in a defendant's box in a courtroom. Others were also scammed as they sought help to acquire visas through unconventional means.

To support her visa application, Susan had to provide proof of how she was going to pay for her studies. This was a difficult challenge to overcome because she couldn't afford to pay for her Master's degree programme herself and had to find a friend or relative who was willing to present his or her bank statements to support her application. After much persuasion from her mum, Susan's uncle (her mum's older brother) agreed to give her his bank statements to use as proof to the consular section at the British High Commission that she could afford to pay for her Master's degree since he was supposed to be sponsoring her studies in the United Kingdom. Her uncle ran his own business, importing used cars from the United States to Ghana and selling them on so he had quite a substantial amount of money going through his account and a healthy bank balance that showed that he could afford to pay for her studies. The real plan was that she was going to work when she arrived in London to pay her way through her studies. Susan's dad had unfortunately passed away during her third year in secondary school, leaving behind Susan, her younger brother, sister and her mum.

After bidding her mum and siblings a tearful farewell at the Kotoka International Airport in Accra and a six-and-a-half-hour flight, she arrived at Gatwick Airport, bubbling with excitement at arriving in the UK. She had to wait for an extra three and a half hours at the arrival hall before her aunt, Tina finally showed up. Well, Aunt Tina was not exactly a blood relation but a good friend of her uncle whose bank details were used in acquiring her student visa. In Ghana, culturally, older family friends and even acquaintances had their names prefixed with the title 'Aunty' or 'Uncle' as a sign of respect. Susan was to stay with Aunt Tina until she found her way around town and got a bit more used to the lay of the land, in terms of how things worked within the UK system.

Driving home from the airport, Aunt Tina was very pleasant as she asked Susan how everyone was doing back at home. At her two-bed flat in Tottenham, North London, Susan met Aunt Tina's two daughters for the first time. Aba was fourteen and Esi was eight. Susan was to share a room with Aba while Esi moved in with her mum. Aunt Tina's husband had moved permanently back to Ghana and had set up his business there. His wife, Aunt Tina, and kids were however not keen about the move and had obviously remained in the UK. Susan was full of appreciation for the sacrifices they were all making for her and was effusive in expressing her thanks to her hosts.

Three weeks after arriving in the UK, Susan found a job at a restaurant as a waitress, earning £7 per hour. She had written to the University to defer her course for a year and was looking forward to working hard to save up for her studies. Her first pay after two weeks of work was paid into Aunt Tina's bank account because she did not yet have the necessary documents to open a bank account in her own name. Aunt Tina was already home when Susan arrived home from work that Friday evening. Excited at the thought of starting saving up for her studies, she went up to her and asked her if the money had been paid.

Well, the honeymoon was over and she was in for a rude shock. Aunt Tina explained to her that since she was working, she had to contribute to the rent, water, gas and electric bills as well as the telephone bill. She either paid her share of the bills or moved out. Susan had assumed that the careless abandon with which one could move in with a relative in Ghana was the same in the UK. Speechless with disbelief, she watched in shock as Aunt Tina gave her half of her pay, telling her that she had put the remainder towards her contribution to the various household bills.

For the next six months, Susan received half of her salary from Aunt Tina each time she was paid and the atmosphere in the house was always tense whenever Susan was at home. She had to reduce the number of times she showered and used the toilet because Aunt Tina threatened to deduct more money from her salary since she was using up a lot of hot water and she never dared put the heating on if she was home alone no matter how cold it got. Although she hardly ever used the landline telephone because she had a 'pay as you go' mobile phone, the weekly deductions Aunt Tina took still included her use of such utilities.

With frustrated anger, Susan planned her move out of the house. The money that she was meant to be saving for her Master's degree was redirected to fund her first rented accommodation in London. She planned everything quite well. She moved in with Victoria, a lady from Kenya she had become quite good friends with at her place of work. They rented a one-bed flat together and she got her salary paid into Victoria's bank account while she waited to have her own bank account opened. Aunt Tina had been unwilling to change any of the names on her utility bills to Susan's name so she was unable to get the requisite documents as proof of address and hence, open a bank account while staying with her.

"But why did you have to wait that long to move out?" Shouted Akua with righteous indignation. "Half of your salary?" I mouthed in disbelief. "That was a total rip-off," Abena chipped in. Sharon just shook her head in silence.

Chapter 2

After almost nine years in the United Kingdom, Susan had still not started her Master's degree; the primary reason for her coming to the United Kingdom. She had instead applied for other short educational programs (which she never got round to attending) that enabled her to renew her students' visa. As a student she could work legally for only twenty hours a week, one important factor Susan was oblivious to when she planned to work to fund her studies.

"I feel depressed when I think of the time that has flown past and the little I have achieved in that period. I wish I could go back to Ghana but how would I explain these past years? I have neither the Master's degree I came here for nor any other certificate to show for it and I don't know anyone who could help me get a job if I went back. As you know, it's extremely difficult to find a well-paid job in Accra without the recommendation of someone already in the industry or someone who knows the people in positions of power. My mum says she's asked enough favours from her brother and refuses to ask him for any more help. I don't have any savings either." Susan shrugged her shoulders despondently and looking dejected, slumped deeper into her chair.

"Cheer up Su!" I interjected. "It's not such a hopeless situation. It's still not too late to do something about what you are going through."

"That's easier said than done," Akua said, cutting in.

"I have been in the UK for seven years, she continued, and I wish I could turn the clock back. I would certainly do things differently. During my first degree at the University of Ghana in Legon, I met a young man called Eric and fell in love. He was a year ahead of me at university and we were so much in love but my mum could not stand the sight of him. She was convinced that the pervasive levels of poverty within Eric's family would make it virtually impossible for him to take care of me and any kids we might have if I married him. I however continued to meet up with him without the knowledge of my mum.

A couple of months after leaving university, my mum introduced me to James, the son of a friend of hers. James had returned to Ghana from the UK to 'find' a wife. He appeared quite taken with me when we met and I must confess I was quite bowled over at the thought of coming to live overseas. With very little explanation to Eric, I dropped him like hot coals and was soon married to James. Eric was heartbroken then but nothing was going to stop me from coming to live in the United Kingdom. Looking back, I must say I am shocked at how callous and cold-hearted I was.

If anyone had told me before I came to the UK that life overseas was not a bed of roses, I would never have believed it. It seemed like the panacea to all my family's problems at the time. I was green with envy whenever my mates at university who could afford to travel overseas during vacations returned with what seemed like lots of money and beautiful clothes. No one came back to talk about the struggle to find jobs and the difficult long working hours one experienced working as cleaners, care workers, factory workers, construction and security workers, you name it! I was also oblivious to the need for a permit to work before coming here. It's difficult to believe how stupid I was. To me, then, coming to live in the UK was the next closest thing to being in heaven.

Somehow, I just foolishly assumed that once the hurdle of getting a visa was crossed, everything else would just automatically fall into place. I can't believe how naïve and gullible I was at the time. Sadly enough, I was not the only one who held that school of thought. Most of my friends were as gullible as I was then and would have given a tooth and possibly an arm to exchange places with me when I told them I was moving to the UK. Ignorance is not an excuse but unfortunately that is the only excuse I have; well, maybe greed as well," continued Akua.

"I came to the UK with a six-month visitor's visa but never returned to Ghana. My husband James came here with a student visa which expired several years ago. We are both illegal migrants now and live like fugitives on the run. If we were in the United States, we would fall into the category of undocumented migrants. I think I prefer that description to being called an illegal migrant. When we get a job, we have to be always alert just in case immigration officials pay a surprise visit to our place of work to validate the immigration status of those working there. We have both been very lucky so far and somehow always get wind of a visit from immigration officials once they are within our respective work premises so we're able to make a quick getaway. When that happens, we are unable to return to that job because our cover is blown. Those who are not so lucky get arrested and sent to detention centres where they are kept for several months and then deported to their home countries or sometimes, they are released and told to report to the UK's Home Office, the government body responsible for immigration, weekly.

Our lack of work permits means we can only find very low-skilled and low-pay work where the questions and investigations are minimal. Although James holds a Master's degree in International Development, he works as a security guard at different hotels in London, working around the clock on numerous shifts in order to make ends meet.

It is easier if you know someone who resides here legally and would not mind you using their name and personal details to work. I have had to leave four jobs with little warning because I got a tip-off that immigration officials were coming in to check the work status of staff at my workplace. I hear of similar stories in other European countries and the USA as well.

One humiliating incident that makes me cringe whenever I remember it, occurred earlier on this year when I had to go and clean a couple of offices in Canary Wharf. I sometimes take on cleaning jobs in the evenings to supplement the income I get as a Care Assistant. I got out of the lifts on the fifth floor that evening with a vacuum cleaner and bumped into four very well-dressed men (three white men and a black man) who looked like they were from an important meeting or were on their way to one. I started to apologize profusely and then as my eyes met the black man, I realized I was looking into the face of my former boyfriend Eric. Oh, how I wished the ground would open up and swallow me with my sweaty face and vacuum cleaner. With my mouth hanging open in shock, I stared at him and he stared right back at me as the doors of the lift slowly closed after they got in.

I stood rooted there after the lift went down several floors, thinking about the choices I had made and continue to make. James and I have two children. Marilyn, who is five and Michael is three and a half."

A wistful smile appeared on Akua's face as she spoke about her children.

"I sent them to live with my mum in Ghana as we couldn't afford child care here and I needed to get back to work. A friend of mine was returning to Ghana and she agreed to take them to my mum for us. I miss them so much.

My mum has now joined the growing number of grandparents in Ghana looking after grandchildren whose parents live abroad."

Akua sighed deeply. There was an impregnable pause as we all sat there, staring at nothing in particular but silently reflecting on our individual lives.

Chapter 3

It however wasn't all gloom and tears. Abena's story was different. In fact it seemed too good to be true but as she later summed up;

"It had all been by the grace of God."

After her first degree at the University of Science and Technology in Kumasi, Ghana, she was awarded a part scholarship to study for an MSc in Management of Information Systems and Digital Innovation at one of the UK's top Universities. Just before completing her Master's programme, she got a job with a leading tech company in the UK that applied for a work permit for her but she had to go back to Ghana to have it processed there. During this period in Ghana, she got married to her childhood sweetheart Ivan who later joined her in the UK.

"Ivan and I have a three-year-old daughter and well, what can I say? Sarah is a lovely girl and we feel so blessed to have her. The greatest thing that has kept me going and helped me through each stage of my life is my belief and faith in Jesus Christ. I have learnt to trust him completely and commit each stage of my life to him and he has never failed me. Of course, there have been challenges and there have been times when I haven't gotten things exactly as I wanted it but I later realized how true it is when the Bible says in Romans 8:28 that 'All things work together for good, to them that love God and are called according to his purpose'. Somehow, whenever things got a bit topsy-turvy in my life, God was always near and walked through with me. I must confess that I feel a bit guilty saying this after hearing Susan and Akua's stories, but I hope sharing this will remind us all about the goodness of God and the need to put our trust in him."

Sharon snickered as Abena carried on, encouraging us to commit our lives to Jesus Christ.

"Are you still caught up in this 'religious stuff' Abena?" Sharon cut in.

"Isn't it about time you got real like the rest of us? You may have gotten a couple of lucky breaks but that's all it's been; lucky breaks! The reality is that life in the UK is tough and it's gotten worse during this recession and for migrants like us, it can be quite punishing.

I was speaking with my cousin in the USA and she shared similar sentiments, claiming that it's even worse over in the States. We are all doing our best to hang in there and not give up. We cannot go back to Ghana empty-handed. We need to have something to show for our years of sojourning overseas. Now, with the current state of the economy, making ends meet is a daily struggle for a lot of people."

"But that is what I have been trying to say Sharon!" Abena said, managing to get a word in after Sharon's tirade.

"I have been there and done all that but it did not work. Trusting in your own abilities to succeed in life does not work. Man's wisdom has failed but what we need is the wisdom of God to push through where there seems to be no way. I know whom I have believed and I am persuaded that he is able to keep all that I commit to him."

"You and those quotations!" Sharon muttered in exasperation, shaking her head and reaching for her now cold cup of coffee.

"Did your Ivan remain faithful to you when he joined you here Abena?" Akua asked. "There are many stories of long-distance relationships going awry when after several years of living apart, the couple are finally united."

"Meeting Ivan is the best thing that happened to me after my accepting Christ as my personal saviour," Abena said in reply.

"Yours must be the exception then," Sharon said. "Most of the stories I often hear of is nothing like you and Ivan."

Akua nodded her head vigorously in agreement as Sharon spoke, leaving us all wondering if James was being unfaithful in their marriage but no one dared ask as what she had opened up and shared with us already was troubling enough.

"I have a friend who moved heaven and earth to get her husband a visa from Togo to join her here. After three refusals at the UK embassy, six months intercessory prayer at a prayer camp in Togo and exorbitant payments to different lawyers, he finally got his visa.

Within six months of arriving in the UK, he had used up the £5000 credit limit on his wife's credit card. The heartbreaking part of it was that he used it to buy clothes for his girlfriend. It infuriates me so much when I hear stories like this." Sharon continued.

"I guess that is why I am still not married. I cannot tolerate such nonsense. I have less heartache concentrating on my career as a doctor. It is stressful enough without the added complication of marital disharmony!"

"Don't be such a cynic Sharon!" I said, finally managing to get a word in.

"Let's push the pause button on the stories of our lives and go find something to eat. I am starving!" After quibbling for a short while on where to go and grab a bite, we finally decided to go to a Thai restaurant that was a couple of bus stops away from where we were. The rain had thankfully stopped as we stepped out but there was an unmistakable chill in the air that had us all clutching our jackets and coats tightly around us for warmth.

Walking to the bus stop was a quiet affair. It was obvious that the preceding subject of conversation had left us all quite pensive and in deep thought.

Thankfully, we didn't have to wait too long before a bus pulled up. The restaurant was only two bus stops away but we didn't bother walking. We piled into the bus, still looking absent minded.

"Hey cheer up girls!" Sharon called to us, trying to put some spark back into the conversation.

"Why the long faces? No one's dead! It's going to be alright. It feels weird being together on the bus after these years. Doesn't it feel like we have sneaked out of school?"

We all burst into laughter. That quip from Sharon got us to forget for a short while, the serious topics of conversation we had been having and got us reminiscing about secondary school again.

Chapter 4

The restaurant was quite packed when we arrived so we had to wait for a couple of minutes before we could get a table for five but eventually, we were seated and our orders placed.

Akua picked up from where she had left of, as we waited for our orders.

"I spend a lot of money buying phone cards to check on my kids in Ghana. Marilyn was two and Michael was just six months old when James and I sent them to Ghana. Can you believe that the last time I called home, Marilyn said I was not her mum?" At this, Akua burst into tears, burying her head into Susan's shoulders. Heavy sobs shook her whole body as her bottled up feelings of pain, regret and anguish poured out. There wasn't a dry eye around the table.

As if on cue, two waiters appeared at our table carrying our various orders of food and doing their best not to appear too curious at the tearful and gloomy faces around the table.

We tried to look interested in the wide array of food displayed before us but it was obvious there was very little appetite for it. As I passed a bowl of spicy chicken curry to Susan, I saw her jaws drop in astonishment as she stared at the doorway. Involuntarily, we all turned to look in that direction. A middle-aged black man and lady had just walked in with their arms around each other and were being shown to a table a couple of tables away from us. They looked pretty ordinary; nothing strange about them.

You would think a horse had just walked in and asked for a table, judging from the look on Susan's face.

Shaking her head and muttering to herself, Susan said.

"I had heard it but did not believe it."

"Heard what?" We all said in unison.

At that, we all burst out laughing. Somehow, the tearful moments of the last few minutes were temporarily forgotten as we all turned to Susan.

"It's a long, complicated story," she started.

"That man who just walked in is Richard. He is married to my friend Femi. Richard is Kenyan and Femi is Nigerian. They met in the UK about four years ago."

As if fearing to be heard, Susan lowered her voice and moved closer to Akua who was sitting next to her.

"The lady he walked in with is Isha who is also Nigerian and Femi's former best friend." "I think I know where this story is heading," Sharon chipped in with a 'wait and see' look on her face.

"When Femi first arrived in the UK, her uncle who had promised to host her was nowhere to be seen. He did not pick any of her calls or respond to any of the numerous messages that she sent him. After spending the night at Heathrow Airport, Femi called her friend Isha. Isha was born in the UK but was sent to Nigeria by her parents after her GCSEs. She stayed in Nigeria and came back to the UK after completing her first degree.

Femi met Isha at university in Nigeria and that's where they became very good friends.

They stayed in touch even after Isha returned to Britain and four and a half years after university, Femi placed an 'SOS' call to Isha from Heathrow airport. With the help of strangers, Femi managed to get on the right sequence of trains to Dagenham, East London, where Isha lived.

According to Femi, Isha was immensely helpful to her. She offered her free accommodation in her one-bed flat until she found a permanent job as a shop assistant, using Isha's identity since she came to the UK as a visitor and was not allowed to work. At work, therefore, Femi was called Isha. It took some getting used to but Femi soon got used to the way things worked. All paperwork and documents that needed signing were in Isha's name. They lived together and got along very well. Femi worked extremely hard. With all the money she had managed to save and some borrowed funds, she paid a Dutch acquaintance £7,000 for a marriage of convenience.

This was to enable her to obtain a resident's permit since her visitor's visa had long expired. A day before their marriage registration, Femi received a text message from her Dutch husband-to-be that he had to respond to a family emergency in Holland and so had had to rush out of the UK. That was the last she heard of this guy.

Unsurprisingly, she was devastated and sank into depression for weeks. Not long after putting this incident behind her, Femi met Richard and fell in love. Richard was also apparently in love. The only hitch to their courtship was that they were both illegal migrants struggling to make ends meet."

"Can you go straight to the point," Sharon cut in. "I am getting a bit tired of this long winding story."

"I told you it was long and complicated," Susan replied. Turning to the others, Susan continued as if she had not been interrupted.

"When Richard and Femi decided to get married, they rented a two-bed apartment with Isha.

The twist in the marriage was that Femi continued to sign all her documents as 'Isha' because she was afraid immigration officials could pay a surprise visit to the registry while she was getting married. It had happened to someone she knew and she was not taking any chances. She planned to have a name change later. Femi's name therefore did not appear on her marriage certificate but stated that Richard was married to Isha.

Isha claimed at the time that she did not mind Femi doing this because she had no intention of ever getting married."

"What!" Screamed Abena.

"Shush Abena. Keep your voice down." Susan whispered.

"When the affair between Richard and Isha started, friends warned Femi but she could not believe this could be happening between her best friend and her husband. The last time I spoke to Femi, she was extremely distraught. She said Isha had moved out of their shared apartment and had given her two months to stop using her identity to work or she would alert immigration officials of her status as an illegal immigrant. Since it's her name on the marriage certificate, she has literally claimed the marriage, and that muppet, Richard is happy to go along with that arrangement because he knows being married to Isha who is British could be his ticket to regularizing his stay in the UK.

I did not believe that Isha could be so heartless and as for Richard, hmmm, I wish I could just shake him until his teeth rattled in his mouth. He is so selfish and just does not care. The saddest part I find in this whole saga is that Femi has a three-month-old baby who she is struggling to take care of. It's all such a mess and now look at Richard and Isha sitting at that table and mooning over each other.

How I would love to wipe that grin off his face," Susan said under her breath.

As if Richard sensed that we were talking about him, he raised his head at that point and looked in our direction. Everyone quickly turned their heads away except Susan who stared right back at him until he turned away.

Chapter 5

We turned to our food once again, each one of us lost in our own thoughts and for about five minutes, the only noise that could be heard from our table was the clanging of cutlery knocking against plates and the slow munching of food.

The silence around the table was suddenly broken by the ringing of Abena's cell phone. It was her husband Ivan and her three-year-old daughter Sarah calling to say good night to her before she was put to bed. Abena was not going home that night since we were all spending the night at Sharon's home. This was a real girls' night out, with no husbands, boyfriends and kids allowed to join in.

Watching Abena as she spoke to her husband and daughter with a sparkle in her eyes and lilt in her voice was quite revealing.

"You truly are happy in your marriage and not just pretending," Sharon burst out, looking quite shocked as she watched Abena come off the phone.

Abena burst into laughter causing the rest of us to join in but Sharon saw nothing funny with the comment that she had just passed, looking genuinely surprised at us for laughing.

"There is so much disappointment and disillusion out there that I can't help but think and believe that marital bliss, to put it lightly, belongs only in fairytales and romance novels."

"Sharon," Abena said still smiling,

"There is no relationship that does not have its challenges. We have had our fair share but going through together has made us stronger and enriched our lives tremendously. Ivan's dad was initially abhorred at the thought of his son marrying me because we come from different tribes in Ghana and don't speak the same indigenous language. They are Ewes and I am an Ashanti and he wanted his son to marry someone from their tribe. For two years he vehemently opposed our relationship and would not even acknowledge my existence when he saw me. We did not want to get married without his blessing so continued to wait and pray until he finally gave in. Now, he is cordial and is gradually thawing in his attitude towards me. This threatened our marriage greatly, especially during our first year together but we have learnt how to deal with it without letting it come between us again. I love my husband and have a wonderful marriage by God's grace."

Sharon stared at Abena in wonder and said,

"Wow, you must be one of the lucky ones. Well, it's quite late now. Let's get going. We have a bit of a trek before we get to my apartment."

After a couple of minutes of discussing the quickest route from Waterloo to East Croydon train station, we decided to get a South Western train to

Clapham Junction and change for a Southern train going through East Croydon.

The journey to Sharon's apartment was another sober affair as we all remained engrossed in our thoughts. After almost an hour and a half and two delayed trains, we reached East Croydon Train Station. We got out of the station just in time to catch a tram on its way to Beckenham Junction. We got off at Sandilands, two stops after East Croydon Station and had to walk another five minutes to get to Sharon's apartment. The rain and slight chill of the afternoon had given way to a build-up of frost and a fall in the temperature to two degrees Celsius. It was almost midnight when we trudged into the apartment, quite exhausted physically and emotionally.

"Wow," exclaimed Akua and Abena as they entered Sharon's two-bed apartment.

It was really spacious and tastefully decorated with no clutter in sight. Sharon had always been very neat and well organised, even in secondary school and that trait had obviously not left her. The modern design in her living room was complimented by a couple of African carvings and wall hangings and the fireplace soon had the room feeling very warm and cozy.

"It's lovely in here as always," I said to Sharon. I had been to Sharon's apartment a couple of times so I was no stranger there but it was the first time Akua, Susan and Abena had visited so they kept on 'oohing' and 'aahing' over the place.

"Anyone interested in a cup of tea or coffee?" Sharon shouted from the kitchen.

"Not yet! I will change first." Akua replied. We all decided to follow suit.

Afterwards, we congregated on the carpet in our nighties and pyjamas cradling cups of tea and coffee and chocolate for me as usual. Sharon joined us in the living room with a cup of coffee and curled up on her sofa. Looking fondly around, she said, "It's really comfortable in here. I love my apartment although I must confess it can get pretty lonely in here sometimes. Most of the time, I am too tired when I get home to think about loneliness. I just grab a snack, have a quick shower and then fall into bed. However, when I am off duty and not hanging out with friends, I get home and the walls of this apartment seem to be screaming out at me in silence. I know this may sound a bit crazy but I sometimes can't stand being in here. When that happens, I just get out of here and go for a jog or a long walk. My parents used to nag me so much about getting married until I broke down on my last visit to Ghana last summer and told them I would not visit again, if they didn't stop going on and on about being still single. The worst part is at family gatherings where aunties and uncles ask when you'll introduce them to their son-in-law and when they will meet their grandchildren.

I've had countless matchmaking attempts and meet-ups that I couldn't turn down because I didn't want to offend the people who were trying to set me up. Most of the men I've met are painfully immature or extremely intimidated by the fact that I am a doctor and would not be able to be 'submissive' as a wife. It's hilarious! Although I am an A&E doctor and not a General

Practitioner, I've seen a rise in stress-related ailments and mental health breakdowns caused by disastrous marriages. I have friends too that tell me about the sexual scandals they or their spouses get embroiled in and I must confess that these make me very wary of the institution called marriage. The divorce statistics is not encouraging either.

Unfortunately, I don't often hear of the lovely stories like Abena shared. Either they are few and far between or those with positive stories to share are not talking about it."

Sharon sighed deeply and stared vaguely at the fireplace, quite lost in her own thoughts.

"Don't you miss being in secondary school where all that one worried about was how edible the food served in the dining hall would be or how you could avoid being sent to run errands by the senior girls in the higher school years?" I said.

We all broke out into laughter and spent the next couple of minutes recounting some of the bizarre ways through which we had tried to outsmart the girls in the senior years when we were juniors in secondary school. As a junior student in the first and second year of secondary school; not just at St Philomena's but in most boarding schools in Ghana, the senior students in their final year were revered, admired and feared. This made running errands for them, weirdly, something that junior students could boast about. However, in as much as junior students felt somewhat honoured to have a senior student show an interest in their school life, they often got fed up with having to run around after them and this often led to carefully and cleverly thought-out schemes to outwit the seniors and avoid the many errands that could come their way, such as washing dishes, clothes, fetching buckets of bath water or making their beds.

Chapter 6

"I know how lonely it can sometimes be as a foreigner living in the UK." I said, curling up closer to the fireplace. I remember when I was studying for my Masters, I spent that Christmas all alone in my room in the halls of residence. A friend of mine who had invited me home for the holidays cancelled at the last minute because her parents were not 'sure' about me and well, couldn't have a stranger at a family gathering. I spent the day crying in my room and had to pretend to my parents that all was fine when they called as I did not want them to worry.

I'm going out now with a white English guy I met on a work trip. We both work in research but thankfully not the same company." I ignored the wide-eyed surprised looks on Akua, Susan and Abena's faces as I opened up about myself.

"The first time I met his family, I was so nervous and self-conscious. I only managed to sip water and messed around with the food on my plate during lunch. His parents tried to make me feel welcome but I could tell they were curious and possibly unsure of the black Ghanaian girl their son was going out with. Stanley did his best to reassure me before I met his parents and younger sister but I couldn't help being nervous. We got through that first meeting eventually and I think they are now slowly getting used to me. My parents weren't any better. The first time I told them I was going out with Stanley and mentioned that he was white, my dad was eating and choked on his food for about two minutes before carrying on in shock. This was over the phone so my mum quickly took the phone from him and asked me to repeat what I had said to my dad to get him to choke."

I chuckled as I remembered the ensuing conversation with my mum and the thousand and one questions, I had had to answer.

"How do you handle your cultural differences?" Susan asked. I laughed and shrugged my shoulders. "It's a huge learning curve but we are taking each day at a time and learning as much as we can about each other as we go along. Loving each other helps to make the challenges more bearable."

We all sighed deeply in unison and then burst into laughter.

"Some of the stories people have to tell of their sojourns overseas are simply mind-boggling. Indeed, it's not surprising that people who have never travelled outside Africa or whichever continent they were born, in search of greener pastures find it hard to believe these stories as they sometimes seem a bit too far-fetched. It is almost as if we exaggerate in order to discourage them from travelling too." Akua said quietly.

"Well, I don't think the issue is with travelling per se but more to do with the sheer ignorance about how the host country operates, including the requirements for work, study and the ensuing general lifestyle change," I said in reply before continuing.

"I know some people in Ghana and other developing countries are selling their possessions to be able to afford to pay middlemen who boast about their abilities to facilitate procuring visas to travel abroad. Some of the most popular destinations are the USA, UK and Canada. Most of the time, these offers of help turn out to be scams and these people lose awful amounts of money that could otherwise have been put to better use as capital for other ventures. The quest for greener pastures has led to so many people making costly mistakes that cannot be easily rectified or reversed.

There are of course, those who have travelled overseas and succeeded in making something of themselves. Someone may argue that success is relative. Your definition of success may not necessarily be mine. Some of our friends from secondary school and university who stayed in Ghana and did not travel overseas have also done very well for themselves. A lot of them are now professionals in very well-paid jobs."

"Well, I guess it's being where God wants you to be," Abena responded.

"I believe that when you are somewhere God has not called you to be, the roadblocks and obstacles that trip you up are many and you could miss out on the blessing he has for you. That's not to say that there would be no obstacles if you are where God has called you to be and it even gets trickier as we start to measure success. Who sets the standard for a successful life? Does a well-paid job or career make you successful, or is a happy marriage or living abroad a criteria for success? Do we have unspoken standards in our minds we are trying to live up to or do we unconsciously compare ourselves with others and beat ourselves for not being where someone else is? Where do we draw the line of contentment? I haven't got any answers either but I guess, that's why we need to press and lean more into God for direction and purpose in this very confusing world."

"Oh Abena! Sharon retorted; do you have to get all religious about everything? What has this got to do with God? This is a matter of right and wrong choices and living with the consequences of these choices."

"But that is the whole point Sharon," Abena replied.

"When you let God influence your choices, you leave very little room for regret later on." Sharon just sighed, rolled her eyes and shook her head in exasperation.

"I sometimes wonder if it would make any difference to people back home and impact the choices they made if documentaries showing what illegal and sometimes even legal migrants go through overseas were to be shown on the various television channels."

Ignoring Abena and Sharon's interruption, I carried on speaking.

"If people were told and shown some of the harsh realities of going to live abroad when you have no legal right to stay and work, would they still make those choices? So many families are affected because of this. There are those who have lived abroad for years and have never gone back to their home countries because they are living overseas illegally and if they went home, they would be unable to return overseas. A lot of people have also got very little to show for their years of sojourning and so are caught between wanting to go back and wanting to stay and build up some savings to act as capital for some kind of business venture back home.

Married couples leave their partners and children in search of greener pastures overseas and are soon gone for fifteen to twenty years. Some never go back home during that period and marriages are left hanging. I have a Congolese friend whose husband travelled to the USA to study. When he left, their two kids were two and four. He has been gone for eight years now and the sad thing is that he hardly contacts them. The last time I spoke to her, she said she had gotten wind that he had married an American lady in order to gain legal residency status and had even had a baby with her. I am not sure if this American lady knows she is being used or if she thinks it is a love match. Sometimes, people come to an agreement and hand over huge sums of money; sometimes, as much as the equivalent of £15,000 to a person who would agree to marriage for a while, well, until the other party also gets the legal right to stay in that country. It's all so complicated. Others who are a bit more cunning are able to convince their 'legal' boyfriends or girlfriends that they are head over heels in love with them and the love lasts until they are able to get what they want from them.

Of course, there are genuine love matches out there, no doubt about that but one gets a bit skeptical if one of the partners is an illegal immigrant and the other is not. I know of another lady in Nigeria whose husband has been in the UK for eighteen years. She had a son with him before he left Nigeria to visit his sister here. She made numerous attempts to join him here but was always refused an entry visa. After about seven years of occasional calls from her husband, she started seeing someone else. The man's family accused her of adultery and called her a harlot anytime they saw her. Her family members have now sent back the drinks, which were presented as part of the customary marriage ceremony, to signal the end of the marriage and have done what is traditionally required to dissolve the marriage but she is still stigmatized for this act of "betrayal"."

"Let's not be too judgemental here," Susan cut in, stopping my tirade.

"I don't think anyone travels overseas with the intention of going to spend the next fifteen or twenty years of their lives there without returning for at least a visit or staying in contact with their immediate or extended family. I believe usually, the plans are either to study, get a good job, save some money and go back home or work for about three to four years, save some money and return home to support their families. It's unfortunate but the sad truth is that a lot of us who travel overseas in search of greener pastures struggle to make ends meet here and hence do not have the means to support their families back home as well. The cost of living in Accra, for example, is extremely high and when you have other dependants such as a wife or husband and kids or you have to look after your parents and/or your other siblings, it can be extremely overwhelming.

My dad died when I was in secondary school and my mum worked extremely hard, selling groceries in the market to look after my siblings and myself. She never remarried but worked tirelessly each day to pay my fees whilst I was at university and my younger brother and sister's fees while they were attending primary and secondary school. She borrowed money from a friend to pay for my airfare when I was travelling here. Now, she is not very well. She has problems with her back and is not able to work as much as she used to do.

I need to support them financially because my siblings are still studying and are not yet in a position to assist financially. I send my mum hundred pounds every two weeks and that goes a long way in meeting a number of expenditures at home. I am not sure if I would be able to support her with that much if I were to be living and working in Ghana. I know a number of well-educated migrants in very low-paying jobs, hardly earning more than the hourly minimum wage but somehow, they are able to save a bit and remit their families back home.

Not everyone who has travelled overseas is irresponsible and has forgotten about their families back home. However, you can get caught in the rat race of life and the persistent drive to get a little bit more; constantly slipping down the greasy poll of success and never managing to touch the prize. I think that is why a lot of people are not able to go back within the time frame they set for themselves. If you earn £300 a week for example, after allowing for deductions for tax, your rent, recurring bills and expenditures, you have practically nothing left. The months and years also quickly go by and it would take a miracle to be able to save enough to even buy a return air ticket back home not to talk about capital to start a business venture upon returning home. Our families back home also need to be a bit more understanding."

Chapter 7

"Life as a foreigner overseas is challenging in a way quite different from the challenges we face back home," Abena said quietly.

"I am saddened at the forgotten ideals and values that we held dear before migrating overseas. The pressures of being an illegal immigrant and the financial constraints that even legal migrants find themselves in often cause them to make certain decisions that are heartbreaking. Unmarried couples cohabiting is now a very common occurrence as it's more cost-effective to do so. Sadly, Christian ideals have been buried and some people would do anything; and I mean anything to get a job or get documents that would allow them to work. I know some of my friends think I am weird because I am always talking about my faith in Jesus Christ but I have come to learn through my little experience that when we allow ourselves to be led by him, we are able to sidestep certain costly mistakes."

"But surely, Abena!" Sharon interjected, "God will understand when a person has to do some of these things you are describing to survive. Some people have families they need to feed and they can't go begging or be left to starve. It's not wrong to want to work, is it? You have not been faced with a situation like that so you might not understand. I think it is alright if you are not hurting anyone in the process."

"Will you say it is alright to lie then?" Abena asked Sharon. "Once you start, you have to keep on telling numerous lies to support the initial one. Where do you draw the line?"

"Oh, will you two just drop it!" Akua shouted, "That subject is too confusing and to be frank, it makes me nervous as well."

Everyone laughed at what Akua said as Abena picked up from where she had left off.

"You may not agree with me but I also firmly believe that not everyone who has migrated here is meant to be here. Some people would have been much better off if they had remained in their countries of origin. A number of illegal migrants in this country end up homeless when family and friends who were helping them initially get fed up with the constant request for assistance.

The son of my parents' neighbours in Kumasi completed his university degree and travelled to the UK on holidays afterwards. He met friends here who convinced him not to go back home at the end of his holiday and has for the last four years been floating in the system as an illegal immigrant working as a customer services assistant in a supermarket during the day and a security guard at night. I am appalled at the terrible waste of knowledge and skill and I am deeply saddened any time I see him.

I always tell him when I see him that I think he is making a terrible mistake remaining here but he just laughs and shrugs his shoulders saying he will go back home next year. I am not exactly sure when that 'next year' will finally arrive. This is just one example of numerous cases of this most disturbing trend. A lot of developing countries have 'brain drain' as one of the numerous problems being faced by their economies. It would have been a bit comforting if these brains were draining into places where they were properly utilized and not just going down the drain."

"If students leaving university and other professionals could easily find gainful employment in their home countries, the attraction to travel overseas to seek greener pastures would be much less." Susan chipped in.

"Hmmm!" I gave a long sigh, echoing the thoughts of despair and helplessness at what was happening around us and our lack of control of the factors affecting uninformed decisions people were taking on a daily basis.

"I wonder if we would do anything differently if we could rewind the clock," I asked.

"I will definitely not repeat certain mistakes I made." Akua replied quickly.

"I hate to say this but if I knew what I know now about life overseas as an illegal immigrant, I would definitely not have dropped Eric like I did in university for a chance to travel here. I may have had the opportunity to travel overseas later on, on my own terms, and been able to return home whenever I wanted instead of the current way I am living. Sometimes, I feel like a fugitive. Some friends of mine in Ghana don't really understand the quagmire I find myself in and tell me to pack up and return to Ghana.

I wish it was as easy as that. My husband is not ready to return anytime soon because he says he has nothing to go back to in Ghana. I haven't either and knowing how much he earns here, there is very little he can do to support our kids and myself if I went back to Ghana. My mum is not helping matters either. She has been complaining for the last couple of weeks that she is not as physically strong as before and can therefore no longer take care of our kids. She is really upset with my husband now because she never got to experience the kind of lifestyle that according to her expectations, befitted someone whose child lives overseas. She calls him names every time we speak on the phone and says she regrets the day I married him. I have managed to prevent him from cottoning onto my mum's name calling but he knows that she disapproves of him now. James lost both parents two years ago and he was unable to attend their funerals because if he left, he would be unable to return to the UK."

What was left of my chocolate drink was half a cup of cold cocoa in no state to be drank. I however still picked up the cup and gently swirling it around, stared intently into it; perhaps hoping for some answers. We were all silent for a while until Susan gave a loud yawn.

"Maybe, it's time we all turned in." Sharon said quietly.

"I am sure the morning will come along with some more cheer and lift this gloomy countenance off our faces."

I gave a quizzical smile and stood with a stretch.

"Who knows what the morning will bring?" I said.

"Who knows!"

We all made a conscious effort to keep the conversation light-hearted the next morning. The previous evening had been emotionally draining and without saying anything, we all steered clear of subjects that would evoke too much emotion.

After breakfast, we hugged each other and bid teary farewells, promising to make more of an effort to stay in touch.

None of us knew that it was going to take an epidemic and much more to get us all together again.

August 2023

Chapter 8

On a bright, dry and sunny Saturday afternoon during August 2023, after fifteen long years, we all finally got together again; this time at Abena's house in the Kent countryside, an hour or so from central London if travelling by train. The world had gone through numerous upheavals including the Covid-19 pandemic, war in Ukraine, political unrest in some nations and a crippling financial crisis that was gripping different nations in different ways; leaving much untold hardship in its wake.

In Ghana where all five of us had migrated from at different points in the year 1999, the country was in the grip of a financial crisis, just like many other nations and this was leading to a large exodus of young professionals outside the country in search of better and greener pastures with the most attractive destinations still the United States, Canada and the United Kingdom. High inflation and a cost-of-living crisis made it difficult for even professionals in relatively well-paid jobs to make ends meet and the number of people living below the international poverty line was on a sharp rise. Although we migrated from Ghana more than two decades ago, we all had close family still living in Ghana and so were fully abreast with most of the news and gossip.

We however made a conscious effort to forget the many worries of the world as we drove up the long drive leading to Abena's house and Sharon drove up right behind me.

There were loud screams of excitement as Akua and Susan got out of my Toyota C-HR and Sharon stepped out of her BMW M Sport. Thanks to the bright warm sunny summer weather, everyone was kitted out in some kind of bright coloured apparel. I was proud of my long sleeveless multicolored African print dress while both Akua and Susan wowed with their jeans and flowery African print tops. Sharon had on a pair of shorts and a halter neck top also in an African print fabric. Abena came out to meet us and she also looked radiant in a bright pink shirt dress with little intricate designs around the sleeve and side pockets.

We hugged each other, exclaiming in disbelief at how time had whizzed past; how different we looked since we last met and whose hair had greyed the most since 2008.

Ivan, Abena's husband and their three kids, fourteen-year-old twins James and Jude and ten-year-old Daniella said a quick hello to us on their way out for the rest of the day. We were to have the house to ourselves; at least till evening. We all waved enthusiastically as Ivan drove out with James sitting at the front next to his dad and Jude and Daniella at the back. There had been a short squabble about whose turn it was to sit at the front with their dad before a decision was made that it was James's turn.

Abena tragically lost her oldest daughter Sarah to a rare genetical disorder when her twin boys were still toddlers and it had been the most challenging time and darkest hours of her life, she said to us later, as we sat together in her lovely sitting room.

"I couldn't bring myself to talk about it for a long time after Sarah passed. I cried for almost a year and nothing Ivan said could console me. I forgot that he was grieving as well and shut everyone out, including him. I couldn't even look after James and Jude and had to get extra help for when Ivan had to be away with work.

I sank into depression and I think for a while, thought it would be better if I died along with Sarah. I asked God 'why' so many times.

A year or so afterwards, around midnight on a Saturday night when I thought everyone was asleep, I crept silently to bed, only to find Ivan still awake and listening to a song on the radio that echoed how bereft I felt and God's presence in the midst of all our hurt and pain. As I listened to the song, I broke down in tears for the hundredth or so time but this time, there was something different about my crying. Crying too, Ivan hugged me tightly and for the first time, I was the one doing the comforting. It felt as if there was a third person there hugging both of us. After that experience, my healing began and I felt I could finally lay Sarah to rest. I still miss her terribly but I know she's safe with Jesus where she will not experience any more pain. Ivan and I got through this by God's grace and mercy and also the support of our church family here. I'm not sure how we would have coped without the love and practical help our friends from church showered on us. Their help meant so much to us, especially because both Ivan and I do not have any other family in the UK."

There was not a dry eye in the sitting room. I blew my nose several times and dabbed at the tears that were flowing freely down my face.

"Why are we always crying when we meet?" Abena said with a laugh; trying to cheer us up after what she had just shared with us.

"Come on, let's go to the kitchen and see what's for lunch. I've made quite a spread."

I blew my nose one more time as we trekked behind her into her very large kitchen with an equally large kitchen island and top of the range appliances and gadgets.

"I love your kitchen." I said to Abena as we sat around the island and she bustled around the kitchen dishing out different kinds of aromatic dishes and turning down any offer of help.

There was jollof rice, (rice cooked in a spicy tomato stew), waakye (rice and black-eyed beans cooked with special brown leaves which turns both the rice and beans dark brown), grilled salmon with potatoes, grilled chicken, beef stew, a mixed vegetable sauce and a large bowl of salad.

"Wow!" we all said as we looked at the mouth-watering spread before us.

"This is amazing, I can't wait to tuck in!" Sharon added.

We dished our food, helped ourselves to drinks and went to the dining room next door to eat.

"It doesn't seem that long since we had a meal together at the Thai restaurant in Waterloo."

Akua started, after sitting down.

"It's shocking to think that it's been fifteen years. I marvel at the twists and turns in life, the choices we make and the consequences that we live with afterwards. I spoke to myself several years ago to stop living with regret and make the best of where I found myself.

I'm no longer married to James.

In 2015, he decided that he could no longer stand the hustle of living in the UK. He wanted us to return to Ghana but I refused to go back with him. We were still illegal migrants at the time and had nothing to show for our years of sojourning if we went back. He left me then and returned to Ghana. He's remarried now.

A year after James left, I found out I was pregnant with a married man I attended church with. I'm not proud of what I did but I was lonely at the time and he promised me so much. I was so mortified and embarrassed when I realized I was pregnant that I left the church without anyone knowing what had gone on while this man carried on attending and serving as an usher. He stopped seeing me when I told him I was pregnant and he threatened to report me to the Home Office if I ever contacted him again. I got in touch with some friends I had in the USA and considered moving there as I thought my chances of making some kind of headway in life there were higher than if I remained in the UK.

This however did not work out so I remained in the UK and barely managed to look after myself and hold down the jobs I was in at the time until I was almost due.

Just before I had my third child, Emmanuel, a friend of mine told me about a Ghanaian man he knew who also had British citizenship and for a fee, would agree to be named as my son's father on his birth certificate and afterwards help apply for British citizenship for my son. I was overjoyed. With the little I had saved and some more I was able to borrow from friends, I paid this man and he kept his word and applied for British citizenship for my son. Thankfully, it was successful. As the mother of a British Citizen, I was also able to regularise my stay afterwards and was miraculously able to later apply for Marilyn and Michael to join me in the UK in 2020."

We all stared at Akua wide-eyed as she continued.

"After being in the UK for over twenty years, I was finally able to return to Ghana on a visit last year to see my mum again. I am so grateful to God that he kept her alive during all these difficult years. She is partially blind in one eye and needs a lot of care now but I am now able to afford a live-in carer for her. I also work with my local council now and although high inflation has led to a cost-of-living crisis in the UK too, I am in a much better position now compared with several years ago. I have to do lots of extra jobs in order to save up to pay a little over £2,500 as visa renewal fees every two and a half years until I have been on that particular category of visa for ten years before I can then apply for indefinite leave to remain in the UK. It's all a bit confusing and sometimes, I am not even sure which of the numerous visa rules apply to me but I'm just extremely thankful that the tables are gradually turning in my favour."

Chapter 9

"You've been through a heck of a lot Akua." Sharon commented quietly.

"I admire your resilience in the face of all these challenges. I am not sure how I would have coped if I were in your shoes. I don't agree with some of the choices you made but like you said earlier on, we make choices and have to live with the consequences.

My life has been pretty straightforward and boring since we last met. I think my family have given up hope of me ever getting married." Sharon carried on with a smirk.

"Having now qualified as an A&E consultant, my plate is quite full with work but after almost dying from Covid in 2020, my outlook on life has changed. Seeing colleagues that I knew fall ill and die and seeing patients die in their numbers although we did all we could to save them was the most harrowing experience I've been through. I was in hospital for almost a month and was on a ventilator for most of the time. My parents were beside themselves with worry as they couldn't travel here and had to rely on one of my cousins to look out for me. Afua was a godsend too and I owe my survival and aftercare to wonderful friends like her.

Now, I take breaks more regularly and travel more when I have the time and pamper myself a bit more too. I am also going out with a doctor friend of mine but not said anything about him to my family as I don't want any pressure from them. We are both being extra cautious and in no hurry to tie the knot. In fact, I think we are both wary of the institution called marriage."

We all laughed at this and paused to have a second helping of the delicious food that Abena had prepared for us.

"I hear there are lots of doctors, nurses and health professionals leaving Ghana now!"

Abena said.

"That's true." Sharon responded.

"A number of my classmates from medical school have in the last five years or so moved to Canada, hoping for a better life and a few have moved to the UK. There's a financial crisis everywhere but for most of those who move, the varied challenging circumstances they encounter when they reach their destinations of choice is still preferable to the financial hardships they faced in Ghana."

"I'm not sure of the process doctors have to go through and the various examinations they have to write before qualifying to practice in countries such as the UK or Canada but I am slightly more familiar with the process nurses and caregivers have to go through to be able to practice in the UK as my sister has been through the mill," Susan said.

"My younger sister, Gloria trained and qualified as a nurse in Ghana about five years ago. She's married with a young son. Last year, she and a couple of other nurses started the visa application process for work permits to work in the UK. They first sat the IELTS exam, which stands for International English Language Testing System. This cost a little over £200 at the time. To progress to the next stage of the application process to work as a nurse in the UK, she needed a score of at least 7.0 while a score of at least 6.0 is required to progress an application as a care worker.

Nurses who after obtaining 7.0 in their IELTS and are able to scale the various hurdles and enter the UK, have the final challenge; an exam called the Objective Structured Clinical Examination (OSCE), a competency test that is part of the Nursing and Midwifery Council's (NMC) registration process for nurses and midwives trained outside the European Union or the European Economic Area.

Gloria scored 6.0, just like a number of her colleagues who sat the exam so although they were qualified nurses in Ghana, they could only apply to be care workers in the UK. After the hurdle of the IELTS, they had to take another exam which is a computer-based testing (CBT) exam. All applicants then had to apply for clearance from the Ghana Nursing and Midwifery Council (NMC) who in turn have to contact the UK NMC to let them know that the applicants are not under any form of study bond or unfulfilled legal obligation to them. This application cost around £140 at the time, after which I believe, they also get a unique registration code.

When all of that is done, then you reach the hardest part, in my opinion. Finding and applying for a job in the UK, following which the prospective employer will apply for a Certificate of Sponsorship (CoS) for the prospective applicant. Apparently, all migrant workers applying for a skilled worker visa need a CoS certificate and have to work specifically for the employing company that applied for the CoS certificate.

Now, here is the twist. Most of the health professionals applying to be care workers and nurses struggle to navigate the UK job application process, thereby creating the need for middlemen and women who are literally fleecing and bleeding prospective applicants dry."

Abena stretched, I yawned, Akua was still eating and Sharon looked on with rapt attention as Susan paused to take a sip of water.

"You always have such long and winding stories Susan," I said with a chuckle.

Susan laughed and carried on.

"CoS contractors are charging nurses several thousands of pounds sterling to provide them with the certificate, linked to a job in the UK. Once this payment is made, the health professional can proceed with their visa application which is then likely to succeed.

Our mouths hanged open in shock as Susan continued.

"A number of the nurses, including my sister are unable to afford to pay the exorbitant fees charged by the middlemen for the CoS certificates and resort to borrowing from banks, selling any assets they may have and loans from friends and family; all in a bid to escape the shores of Ghana. For some of the applicants, this feat of mobilizing thousands of pound sterling to pay their way is not achievable so the 'CoS contractors', knowing the tricks of the trade then play their final card. Since the visa allows the applicant to travel with a dependant; a 'husband' or 'wife' who is able to afford to pay several thousands of pound sterling as well is found for the applicant in order to speed up the process. In these cases, the legitimate spouses are therefore left behind and if everything went to plan, the couple would go their separate ways upon arriving in the UK."

"Eiiiii! 3den As3m ni!" (meaning, what kind of problem is this), I exclaimed in Twi (a language spoken by the Akan tribe in Ghana).

Susan carried on, ignoring my exclamation in Twi.

"What's even more upsetting is that some of the nurses, who arrive in the UK as care workers are able to work for only a few months and then informed by the companies that issued their CoS certificates that there are no more employment opportunities. This leaves them unemployed with no skilled worker visa to find another job. They then have to find some other way to earn an income to pay middlemen for another CoS certificate. This has left many nurses who enter the UK as care workers stranded and desperate for any kind of work to raise money to keep on paying for CoS certificates.

It's all a very expensive, complicated and daunting process, especially if you have no one guiding you through it and those who claim to be helping are like wolves in sheep's clothing. Apparently, some of these applicants have no health care experience or qualification but are assured of visas and UK jobs by the 'CoS contractors' if they are able to pay the huge sums of money requested.

Our hospitals in Ghana are emptying of health professionals at an alarming rate and I wish the Ghanaian government would realise this and do more to keep them after they have received their training. What's worse is, as we've said before, a number of these professionals work in areas that do not utilize their full skillset."

We all sighed deeply as we individually meditated on our various motivations for migrating to the UK. Hadn't we all come here in search of greener pastures like other Ghanaians were doing now? Did we have any moral right to tell them not to leave Ghana or were we by the very nature of the lives we were living now proving the theory right that it paid to leave the shores of our country for a better life in the West? Would it be right to encourage our friends and family to stay back and build our country when we ourselves had left the country?

We all stared at nothing in particular, but remained in deep thought for several minutes.

Chapter 10

"Gloria has left her son and husband in Ghana and is now in the UK as a care worker."

Susan carried on, as if there hadn't been a pause.

"She's been lucky to stay in work but after paying her rent and utility bills, there's practically very little left to send back home to her husband who is a teacher and her son. I tried to talk her out of coming to the UK but she wouldn't have any of it. She travelled here with a very good friend of hers called Esi who is also a nurse, entering the UK as a care worker and their two so-called "husbands". They have no idea where those men are now.

Esi left her real husband in Ghana with their two children; the eldest child only nine years old, hoping to work and earn enough to transform the lives of her family back home in Ghana. Two months after arriving in the UK and starting her care work, Esi found out she was pregnant with her third child. She was devastated and heartbroken especially when a couple of months down the line, she started showing and was sacked from her job for health and safety reasons. Friends advised her to abort the baby when she found out she was pregnant but she couldn't bring herself to do that. She's now heavily pregnant, homeless and does not qualify to receive any help from her local council as her entry visa stated that she had no recourse to public funds. This simply means she's not entitled to any benefits. She's a mental wreck now and always crying, unable to return to Ghana because of the huge debt she says she left behind after borrowing to fund the various applications and airfare. Her friends cannot help her as they will not be permitted to house a pregnant woman in the rooms that they are renting. The only support she is currently receiving is from a homeless charity that operates from a church close to where she used to live.

I met her a couple of days ago and tried to convince her to return to Ghana but she was horrified at the thought and adamant that going back to Ghana was not an option for her.

It's so sad. I keep on thinking about her and wondering what will happen to her.

I returned to resettle in Ghana in 2015 after my renewed student visa expired again. I never got round to studying for my Master's Degree. I was at the end of my tether here. Nothing was working for me. I could barely afford to pay my rent and bills and my mum was very sick. I called my uncle who helped me with his bank statement to get a visa to travel here and told him the plight I was in. He promised to speak with a friend he had about finding a job if I returned home. I borrowed the money to buy my airfare and was on the next flight back to Accra. I interviewed for a role as a Junior Partnership Facilitator at the Ministry of Foreign Affairs in Ghana when I returned and got the job towards the end of 2015.

The circumstances around travelling in search of greener pastures differ from person to person but for me, the best thing I did for myself was return to Ghana after sixteen years of groping around in a maze in the UK.

My mum passed away in 2020, during the Covid-19 pandemic and I am thankful to God that I could spend a few years with her before her passing. I wouldn't have had that if I stayed in the UK. I have a better quality of life now in Ghana and will be getting married at the end of the year, just before Christmas, as you already know. I am currently on a work trip to the UK and will be returning to Ghana next week."

I gave Susan a hug and whispered 'congratulations' to her.

"We are very proud of you Susan," Abena added quietly.

"Life is full of different twists and turns, highs and lows and it's important that we don't remain down with the challenges but pick ourselves up, dust ourselves down and carry on. Esi's story is terribly sad but after what she went through to be able to enter the UK, I'm not surprised she's refused to return to Ghana. As you go back to Ghana next week, I wish you the best with everything and pray God's blessing over you and your fiancé."

We all jumped as Akua's phone rang shrilly. We got up to help Abena clear up the plates and remaining food as Akua answered her phone call.

"Come out onto the patio." Abena called out.

We moved out, each one of us, carrying a drink of some sort.

Out on the patio, there were cushioned garden chairs, a round table with a parasol in the middle, overlooking a carefully manicured lawn with colorful flower beds at each corner of the long rectangular garden.

"It's so serene and peaceful out here." I said to Abena.

"I love the countryside but my husband Stanley prefers the bustle of the city so we've both compromised and met each other halfway. It's neither too busy nor too quiet where we live now. I was going out with Stanley when we last had our reunion in 2008 but we broke up a year later and got back together after several months. We broke up a second time, got back together again and finally decided to get married in 2015. It's been an interesting rollercoaster since then." I said with a wistful smile on my face.

We travelled to Ghana to meet my family before our wedding and had a wonderful holiday there. It was Stanley's turn to be nervous when we were going to meet my parents but he realized later that it was unfounded. My dad asked him a couple of very pointed questions which he answered quite well. I remember my reluctance to leave the two of them together at the time but my mum pulled me away and I waited nervously for the interrogation to be over. My dad was all smiles when they finally joined my mum and I for lunch and Stanley's wink and thumbs-up behind my dad when he saw the questioning look on my face was such a huge relief.

We've been trying for a baby for the last five years but have been unsuccessful so far. We decided to undergo IVF treatment but that was also unsuccessful."

I quickly looked down as tears rolled down my face involuntarily. Sharon and Abena both put their arms around me and Susan rubbed the back of my hand while Akua looked on helplessly, unsure of what she could also do.

"I've had two miscarriages during this time and it's been tough but Stanley has been an amazing support during this period. He broached the subject of adoption earlier on this year but I'm not sure I'm ready for that step yet.

Anyway, enough of sob stories."

I wiped my face, jumped to my feet and put on a brave smile.

"The important thing is we have all pulled through various challenges in the last fifteen years. Time and life has happened to us all but we are fighters and survivors. Nothing can get us down."

This seemed like such a poor attempt at a motivational speech, even to my own ears but I had nothing better to say. Abena came to my rescue.

"Despite the many challenges that we've all been through, God has been there for us all. I believe that this side of eternity will always have its uncertainties and troubles but having faith in Jesus Christ and the reassurance of eternal life through him should strengthen us and give us hope. Worldly institutions seem to be crumbling around us. World economies are struggling to stay afloat and the search for a better world; so called greener pastures has led to mass migration around the globe. Millions of people have had to flee their homes because of wars, terrorist attacks, famine, natural disasters; you name it! It seems as if the whole world is in transit. The UNHCR recently estimated that over 110 million people have been forcibly displaced from their homes with over 36.4 million refugees around the world so far this year. We are all searching for something to fill the void deep down in our hearts. I believe that only Christ can fill that void; that emptiness.

Money, Power, Status, Sex and all that trails in its wake can never be the answer, though many have tried to use that.

I don't know what tomorrow holds but I know who holds tomorrow and I am confident that he is able to keep that which I commit to him."

This time, there were no retorts or snide comments about Abena's talk about her faith and beliefs. Even Sharon was quiet. We all sat there quietly in deep thought; watching the sun turn into a beautiful golden ball of fire as it slowly set behind the white and pink looking clouds. The artistic display of colour in the sky was a sight for sore eyes and it took the whirring sound of the house gates sliding open and Ivan driving in with their kids to make us realize how late it was.

"We better get going." I said, as I stood up. "Hopefully, we will not have to wait another fifteen years before we meet together again."

Everyone laughed.

"Who knows, the next time we meet again, we might all be back in Ghana," Sharon added to more laughter.

After a teary farewell and lots more hugs, we drove out, still waving at Abena and Ivan who had joined his wife outside to see us off.

The sun was now almost fully hidden behind the pink clouds as we drove out and watching the clouds meet the horizon suddenly filled me with hope. Smiling broadly, I sat up with a straight back behind the steering wheel and stepped fully on the accelerator.

Author's Profile

Copyright Evrim Ozarslan, PhotoSmile

Nana Ama Adu-Kwapong is a journalist who lives in the United Kingdom with her husband and three children. She holds an MSc in Gender, Development, and Globalisation from the London School of Economics and Political Science, a BA in English with Philosophy from the University of Ghana, and a Diploma in Journalism from the Ghana Institute of Journalism. For the last eight years, she has volunteered with a charity that supports refugees, asylum seekers, and homeless people in London.